STANDUP SHAKESPEARE

Words by
SHAKESPEARE

Music by
RAY LESLEE

Book by
★ KENNETH WELSH

★

DRAMATISTS
PLAY SERVICE
INC.

STANDUP SHAKESPEARE was produced by The Folger Shakespeare Library (Werner Gundersheimer, Director; Janet Alexander Griffin, Producer) at The Folger Elizabethan Theatre, in Washington, D.C., on March 18, 1994. It was directed by Ray Leslee; the musical arrangements were by Jack Bashkow and Ray Leslee; the technical production was by William Fecke; the production coordinator was Susanne Oldham; the musical direction was by Jack Bashkow; the vocal arrangements were by Thomas Young; the puppet was by Marthe Jocelyn; and the stage managers were Russell Kaplan and Jon Radulovic. The cast was as follows:

THE FOOL...David Margulies
FEMALE SINGER ....Alison Fraser
MALE SINGER..Thomas Young
HECKLER ....Brad Waller
PIANIST ....Ray Leslee
WOODWINDS...Jack Bashkow
VIOLIN ....Rob Thomas
BASS ....Dave Dunaway

STANDUP SHAKESPEARE was produced by the Shubert Organization (Gerald Schoenfeld, Chairman) and presented at Theatre 890, in New York City, on March 24, 1987. It was directed by Mike Nichols; the set design was by John Arnone; the costume design was by Cynthia O'Neal; the lighting design was by Mitchell Bogard; the sound design was by Barbara Schwartz; the musical direction was by Ray Leslee; the vocal arrangements were by Thomas Young and the production stage manager was Zane Weiner. The cast was as follows:

THE FOOL..Kenneth Welsh
FEMALE SINGER ....Tabore Johnson
MALE SINGER..Thomas Young
PIANIST ....Ray Leslee
WOODWINDS...Jack Bashkow
VIOLIN ....Marshall Coid
BASS ....Dean Johnson

STANDUP SHAKESPEARE was produced by the West Bank Cafe (Steve Olsen, Rand Foerester, Lewis Black and Rusty Magee, Producers) and presented there, in New York City, on April 23, 1984 through April 23, 1988. The casts were as follows:

THE FOOL..Kenneth Welsh
FEMALE SINGER ....Sharon Scruggs, Karen Trott
MALE SINGER..Thomas Young, Gilbert Price
HECKLER ....David Purdham, Dan Southern
PIANIST ....Ray Leslee
WOODWINDS...Jack Bashkow, Aaron Heick
VIOLIN ....Paul Woodiel
BASS ....Ratso Harris, Rufus Reid

ACKNOWLEDGMENTS

Mary Ann Anderson

Robin Becker

Glenn Close

Sam Cohn

Sinead Cusak

Robert Duvall

Saul Elkin

Dee Fetters

Manny and Rosalind Fruchter

John Martin Green

Janet Griffin

Werner Gundesheimer

Jeff Hairston

Baxter Harris

Jeremy Irons

Evan Morris

Mike Nichols

Suzanne Oldham

Tom Palumbo

Virginia Penta

Peter Piccirilli

Robert "Bub" Rosen

Howard Rosenstone

Gerald Schoenfeld

Lorraine Shemesh

Christine Shreeve

Jacob and Shirley Simon

David Singer

Dan Southern

Kent Thompson

Karen Trott

Young Audiences (NY)

INTRODUCTION

In the long history of Shakespearean performance, *Standup Shakespeare* is surely unique. It is not only one of a kind in form, but in its success in hitting targets often aimed at and often missed. In both word and music, its relationship to its source is far from reverential, yet somehow entirely comfortable. It proffers real wit and wisdom in place of schlock comedy and pomposity. Its tone is contemporary and populist, but never cheap or condescending. At unexpected moments, its texture, which is basically that of a light, wistful entertainment, turns nappy and deep, and we're in places that only Shakespeare and a few others have known how to reach.

The piece sprouted from the soil of everyday performance, from the search for practical solutions to specific theatrical problems. The present text is the work of Kenneth Welsh, a fine and experienced Broadway actor with many Shakespearean roles to his credit in Stratford (Ontario) and in leading American theatres. Like many actors, Mr. Welsh rummaged through the thespian trunk for ways to make Shakespeare's words strike through with the clarity and impact of a here-and-now experience, and still preserve the integrity of our language's richest stage poetry, with all its syntactical and historical complexities. He was adventurous in his choice of venues, being the sort of fellow who would set up a booth at a Renaissance Fair or gather a crowd around the Bard's statue in Chicago's Lincoln Park, there to vend soliloquies and sonnets and take requests for Shylock or Richard III from chance passersby. He became, in short, a contemporary exemplar of the ancient oral traditions — bardic recitation, strolling mummery — that lie behind Western dramatic literature.

Meanwhile, composer and keyboard performer Ray Leslee was running his own course as Shakespearean populist. As co-founder of a free, outdoor Shakespeare festival in Buffalo, New York, he was involved in many aspects of production over a period of fifteen seasons. This included creating adaptations of the plays for audiences that had no previous experience of live theater and scant background in literature of any kind, let alone an acquaintance with Shakespeare. Thus, there was an *A Midsummer Night's Dream* set in the Hollywood Hills, with a Marx Brothers Puck and a Rogers/Astaire Titania and Oberon ("the King and Queen of *our* fantasy," says Leslee). And there was *The Taming of the Shrew* as a Lina Wertmueller film (remember *Swept Away?*).

But above all, there was Ray Leslee's music, in a wild variety of contemporary styles, and echoes of older ones too. Music as a component of spoken theater has been so downsized in our time that contemporary playgoers may find it surprising that songs of sufficient quality to lead independent lives can emerge from everyday production circumstances, let alone enough of them to comprise a full-length show. True, classical music buffs are aware of much splendid music that has survived on its own, like the many beautiful Shakespeare songs from the times of Purcell and Arne down to ours, or the brilliant suites drawn from incidental music like those for Ibsen's *Peer Gynt* (Grieg) or Daudet's *L'Arlesienne* (Bizet).

This music survives, though, in concert-hall settings, detached from the plays. From my own early New York play-going days, I can recall the use of Mendelssohn's *A Midsummer Night's Dream* music by the Old Vic, and of Lully's for *Le Bourgeois Gentilhomme* by the Comédie Française — live, not recorded, and with both music and actors unamplified. That was in the 1950s, and the productions were considered throwbacks then. Long gone are the days when full orchestras occupied theater pits to render elaborate scores by composers of real importance. The extensive music-theater scores that became standard for hundreds of productions from the late 17th-Century into the 19th — complete with entr'actes, underscoring, dances, songs of all descriptions, and even entire singing characters — have been largely lost, some never published or only incompletely written down, like many of our musical comedy scores. We are left with only the unavoidable songs, a few plinks and plunks for the "magical" moments, perhaps a De Millean brass flourish or two for the history plays, and here and there some electronic wheezings.

With the possible exception of costuming, nothing so fixes a theater piece in period as its music. This explains both why so many composers faced with Shakespeare have adopted a faux Elizabethan tone, and why so many of the fine old scores are a poor fit for modern production. Faced with his particular set of production and audience requirements, Leslee — like Welsh with his open-air declamations — forsook an assumed tone and attitude in favor of an immediate, contemporary connection between text and audience. "I just looked on Shakespeare as my lyricist partner who happened to be dead," he explains. "Between us, we had to make the gig work." And by making the gigs work, Leslee created the musical materials for what eventually became *Standup Shakespeare.*

Welsh and Leslee first met at a New Year's Eve party in 1984, where both participated in a jam session (Welsh is an accomplished jazz trumpeter). Not long after, when Welsh was asked to do a solo evening at New York's West Bank Cafe, he remembered the composer with the Shakespeare songs, and the two began collaborating on the act that grew into *Standup Shakespeare.* At first, this was simply an alternation of songs and recitation. But as Welsh worked on the text — drawing line sequences from everywhere in the canon to create fresh and delightfully apt juxtapositions, entering into bantering exchanges with the singers and musicians — a shaped continuity developed, centered in the character of The Fool.

The Fool has much in common with the rustics, mechanicals, and clowns of the plays. But he is no pratfallen buffoon. He plays on words, he philosophizes with wit and irony. His discourse has a wry, self-deprecating tone, at once resigned and ever-hopeful. He speaks simply, yet with a real sophistication. He seems to draw lessons from experience, but despite the mounting negative evidence he tirelessly renews his romantic quest: to paraphrase another fine lyricist, he falls in love with love and plays The Fool. At moments, a deep melancholy pierces his amusing, rueful surface, for as with any true Shakespearean character, the tragic sense and the comic perspective are at one within him. By the time he has completed his journey, we are genuinely sorry to lose his company and that of his musical companions. We leave the theater aware that we've been in touch with the deepest matters of mind and heart.

The text and music of *Standup Shakespeare* cannot be fully appreciated without each other. Fortunately, the songs (with just enough of the spoken text to give a hint of the combined flavors) are available on CD (Bard BDCB-9509), performed by singers and players long associated with the show. Some of the settings are interpretively surprising. The opening *Tomorrow is St. Valentine's Day,* for example, is very far from the usual Ophelia-esque plaint. But such surprises are explained by the production concepts for which they were created (in this case, Joseph Papp's *Naked Hamlet*), as is the presence of two of the sonnets, incorporated into the plays in Leslee's adaptations.

The big surprise of the music, though, is its sustained level of melodic invention, harmonic texture, and rhythmic variety, and its triumphant blending of apparently ill-matched elements into a plausible, emotionally satisfying whole. To command a range of idioms is admirable in a composer; to actually speak compellingly in each is the real trick, and that is what Leslee has accomplished.

As for the spoken text, it is here, in the following pages.

— Conrad L. Osborne

CONRAD L. OSBORNE, a performer, voice teacher, and critic, has contributed essays, articles, and reviews to *The New York Times, The Financial Times* (London), *High Fidelity/Musical America,* and many other publications. He is also author of the novel *O Paradiso,* and contributor to the Metropolitan Opera's *Encyclopedia to Recorded Opera* and *Encyclopedia to Opera Videos.*

PRODUCTION NOTES

The text was created by taking lines from anywhere in the Shakespeare canon in order to serve the immediate needs of the action. The "game" of finding a line to express a new idea could continue during rehearsal — even performance — anything that helps STANDUP SHAKESPEARE to be real, spontaneous, and provocative is good. As for the music, the songs are basically straight settings of the original lyrics in modern musical styles. The songs are presented in concert-like moments. There are many opportunities for individual expression — the players have extensive solo sections and the singers interpret some of the greatest lyrics ever written.

THE SUCCESS OF STANDUP SHAKESPEARE DEPENDS UPON:

1. A clear and simple understanding of EVERYTHING that is said or sung — in the same way as any modern nightclub comedian or singer would perform.

2. Actors are playing THEMSELVES. Note that there are no character names in the script.

3. A concert setting is the right approach. The show is happening in the same place the audience inhabits — it must not be an "invented" world — as tempting as it is to try and create one. Stools, instruments, equipment and especially MICROPHONE STANDS to "center" and help define a contemporary style of communicating. This is not a "play" or "cabaret" in the traditional sense. The audience must feel they are here with the players.

4. The costumes are the "clothing" of the performers — casual, well-dressed, elegant, comfortable, fashionable and fun. Tuxedos are possible for the musicians. The comedian can be dressed down — even funky — in the same manner that that actor might actually appear in a comedy club. HE'S NOT A JOKE.

5. The lighting must not make unnecessary dramatic demands — yet there are many opportunities to enhance the changes in musical styles from song to song. That is different than coloring the emotional changes during the evening. A cyclorama might work — depending on the size and type of theatre.

STANDUP SHAKESPEARE is meant to be a vehicle for extraordinary talents. The production must trust that, and the fact that the audience will delight in simply hearing these familiar words in a way that they never heard before.

Ray Leslee and Kenneth Welsh, 1996

MUSICAL NUMBERS

1. St. Valentine's Day (Intro)
1A. St. Valentine's Day
2. Shallow Rivers
3. By Gis
4. Say that She Rail
5. Sigh No More
6. I Will Tarry
7. Jazz
8. Let Her Go Hang
9. Come Away Death
10. When in Disgrace
11. I Know a Bank
12. I Do Love Thee
13. How Should I Your True Love Know
14. Take O Take
15. If Music Be the Food of Love Bit
16. Puck
17. O Mistress Mine
18. Let Me Not
19. That Time of Year
20. Shall I Compare Thee
21. Love is Perjured
22. Hey Ho Underscore
23. Hey Ho

STANDUP SHAKESPEARE

(Music #1: St. Valentine's Day — Vamp)

FOOL. *(Enters with band, speaks over vamp.)* I am a fellow of the strangest mind in the world ... I am fortune's fool, and that they know full well that gave me leave to speak. Methinks sometimes I have no more wit than a Christian or an ordinary man has, but I am a great eater of beef, and I believe that does harm to my wit.... I pray you, do not mock me. I am a poor player that struts and frets his hour upon the stage and then is heard no more.... Whence come you, the forest of Arden? I jest, I do but jest ... and ... 'tis my vocation, and 'tis no sin for a man to labor in his vocation ... but, to deal plainly, I fear I am not in my perfect mind ... methinks I should know you *(Points to someone in the house.)* ... and know this man *(Points to someone else.)* ... but I am mainly ignorant what place this is ... and all the skill I have remembers not these garments, and I know not where I did lodge last night.... I'm glad I was up so late, for that's the reason I was up so early. But ... all for your delight, we are not here.... So ... think, when we talk of horses, that you see them ... into a thousand parts divide one man, and make imaginary puissance ... *(Pronouncing the word in different ways.)* pew ... puissance ... puissance. Oh, what's in a name? To show our simple skill, that is the true beginning of our end ... I like this place, and willingly could waste my time in it ... I go, I go, see how I go ... *(Music ends.)* I had rather be any kind of thing than a fool ... I am indeed not a fool, but a corrupter of words, and there is nothing either good, or bad, but thinking makes it so ... Ladies and gentlemen, please welcome, Standup Shakespeare!

(Music #1A: St. Valentine's Day)

MALE SINGER, FEMALE SINGER and PIANIST.
    TOMORROW IS ST. VALENTINES DAY
    ALL IN THE MORNING BETIME

FEMALE SINGER.
>AND I A MAID AT YOUR WINDOW
>TO BE YOUR VALENTINE

ALL THREE.
>THEN UP HE ROSE AND DONNED HIS CLOTHES
>AND OPENED UP THE CHAMBER DOOR.

FEMALE SINGER.
>LET IN THE MAID
>AND THEN THE MAID

ALL THREE.
>NEVER DEPARTED MORE

FEMALE SINGER.
>NEVER DEPARTED MORE

ALL THREE.
>NEVER DEPARTED MORE

FEMALE SINGER.
>NEVER DEPARTED MORE

(Recorder solo.)

ALL THREE.
>NEVER DEPARTED MORE

FEMALE SINGER.
>NEVER DEPARTED MORE

(Repeats.)

(Music #2: Shallow Rivers)

MALE SINGER.
>LIVE WITH ME AND BE MY LOVE
>AND WE WILL ALL THE PLEASURES PROVE

THAT HILLS AND VALLEYS, DALES AND FIELDS,
AND ALL THE CRAGGY MOUNTAINS YIELD
THERE WE WILL SIT UPON THE ROCKS
AND SEE THE SHEPHERDS FEED THEIR FLOCKS
BY SHALLOW RIVERS TO WHOSE FALLS
MELODIOUS BIRDS SING MADRIGALS

FOOL.   I was adored once, too.

FEMALE SINGER.   I had rather hear a dog bark at a crow than a man swear he loves me.

FOOL.   Thou sticks't a dagger in me.

FEMALE SINGER.   Men have died from time to time, and worms have eaten them, but not for love.

FOOL.   The tongues of mocking wenches are as keen as is the razor's edge invisible.

MALE SINGER.   And that's true, too.

(Music #3: By Gis)

FEMALE SINGER.   I must be cruel, only to be kind.

FOOL.   Mock me mercifully, for I do love thee cruelly.

FEMALE SINGER.
   BY GIS AND BY ST. CHARITY
   ALACK, AND FIE, FOR SHAME!
   SOME MEN WILL DO IT, IF THEY COME TO IT;
   BY COCK, THEY ARE TO BLAME.
   QUOTH SHE, "BEFORE YOU TUMBLED ME,
   YOU PROMISED ME TO WED."
   "SO WOULD I HAD DONE, BY YONDER SUN,
   AND THOU HADST NOT COME TO MY BED"
(Musical break.)
   AND THOU HADST NOT COME TO MY BED
(Repeats.)

FOOL.   Was ever woman in this humour wooed? Was ever woman in this humour won? She has a good face, speaks well, and has excellent good clothes.

13

FEMALE SINGER.   Are you honest?

FOOL.   Every man has his fault and honesty is mine.

FEMALE SINGER.   To be honest as this world goes is to be one man picked out of ten thousand.

FOOL.   I have everything an honest man should not have and what an honest man should have — I have nothing.

FEMALE SINGER.   You are more and more a cat.

FOOL.   Are you my bird?

FEMALE SINGER.   I mean to shift my bush, and then pursue me as you draw your bow ... I knew you at the first you were a moveable.

FOOL.   Why, what's a moveable?

FEMALE SINGER.   A joint stool.

FOOL.   Thou hast hit it. Come sit on me!

FEMALE SINGER.   Farewell dear heart, I must needs be gone. Thou art an old love monger. *(Exits.)*

FOOL.   I am amazed and know not what to say.

MALE SINGER.   Not without cause.

PIANIST.   Here's mettle more attractive.

MALE SINGER.   She'll give me for my pains a world of sighs.

FOOL.   Oh, fie.

MALE SINGER.   She'll wish that heaven had made her such a man!

FOOL.   The old saying is no heresy that hanging and wiving goes by destiny. And he that comforts my wife is the cherisher of my flesh and blood.... And he that cherishes my flesh and blood loves my flesh and blood.... He that loves my flesh and blood is my friend ... ergo.... He that kisses my wife is my friend.... No?

MALE SINGER.   A horned man's a monster and a beast. My bounty is as boundless as the sea; My love as deep. Oh, how I long to have some chat with her.

(Music #4: Say That She Rail)

PIANIST.

    SAY THAT SHE RAIL?

    SAY THAT SHE RAIL?

    SAY THAT SHE RAIL, RAIL, RAIL, RAIL?

    SAY THAT SHE RAIL?

FOOL.

>SAY THAT SHE FROWN?
>
>SAY THAT SHE FROWN?
>
>SAY THAT SHE FROWN, FROWN, FROWN, FROWN?
>
>SAY THAT SHE FROWN?

MALE SINGER.

>I'LL GIVE HER THANKS.
>
>I'LL GIVE HER THANKS.
>
>I'LL GIVE HER THANKS, THANKS.
>
>I'LL GIVE HER THANKS.
>
>AND I'LL WOO HER WHEN SHE COMES.
>
>I'LL WOO HER WHEN SHE COMES.
>
>I'LL WOO HER WITH SOME SPIRIT WHEN SHE COMES.
>
>SAY THAT SHE RAIL.
>
>SHE, SINGS AS SWEETLY AS A NIGHTINGALE.
>
>SHE, LOOKS AS CLEAR AS MORNING ROSES.

FOOL and PIANIST:

>IF SHE WON'T BE WED?
>
>IF SHE WON'T BE WED?
>
>IF SHE WON'T BE WED, WED, WED, WED?
>
>IF SHE WON'T BE WED?

MALE SINGER.

>I'LL GIVE HER THANKS.
>
>I'LL GIVE HER THANKS.
>
>I'LL GIVE HER THANKS, THANKS.
>
>I'LL GIVE HER THANKS.
>
>AND I'LL WOO HER WHEN SHE COMES.
>
>I'LL WOO HER WHEN SHE COMES.
>
>I'LL WOO HER WITH SOME SPIRIT WHEN SHE COMES.
>
>SAY THAT SHE RAIL.

FOOL.   Here comes the lady. How now my heart, did you never see the picture of we three?

FEMALE SINGER.   Honey, Milk, and Sugar.... There's three ...

MALE SINGER.   Wilt thou have me, lady?

FEMALE SINGER.   No, my lord. *(Aside.)* To see him kiss his hand and how most sweetly he will swear. Ah, heavens, it is pathetical. *(To Male Singer.)* Your praises are too large. Speak low if you speak love. Your grace is too costly to wear every day.

MALE SINGER.   A pleasant spirited lady. She's too rough for me. *(He exits.)*

FOOL.   I'LL WOO HER WITH SOME SPIRIT WHEN SHE COMES ...

FEMALE SINGER.   Ominous, ominous.... Men are April when they woo, December when they wed. *(She goes over to an audience member and "visits" ... says hello, reads the program, etc.)*

FOOL.   She speaks yet she says nothing. What of that? Her eye discourses. I will answer it.... Two of the fairest stars in all the heavens; Her eyes in heaven would through the airy regions stream so bright that birds do sing and think that it were not night.... See how she leans her cheek upon her hand? Oh, that I were a glove upon that hand, that I might touch that cheek!

FEMALE SINGER.   I wonder you will still be talking, Signor.... Nobody marks you.

FOOL.   She gives me the leer of invitation.

FEMALE SINGER.   This is the silliest stuff as ever I heard.

FOOL.   I do spy some marks of love in her ... lady, thy beauty doth make me like thee well.

FEMALE SINGER.   Will you write me a sonnet in praise of my beauty?

FOOL.   In so high a style that no man shall come over it.

FEMALE SINGER.   To have no man come over me?

FOOL.   Lady, shall I lie in your lap?

FEMALE SINGER.   No, my lord.

FOOL.   I mean, my head upon your lap.

FEMALE SINGER.   Ay, my lord ...

FOOL.   Do you think I meant country matters?

FEMALE SINGER.   I think nothing, my lord.

FOOL.   That's a fair thought to lie between maid's legs.

FEMALE SINGER.   Away you three inch fool!

FOOL.   Am I but three inches? Well, for my own part, look you, I'll go pray ... *(As he exits.)* Where's Dick Surgeon? Fetch Dick Surgeon ...

FEMALE SINGER.   This king comes to kill my heart. My double heart for his single one.... Call me what instrument you will,

(Music # 5: Sigh No More)

though you can fret me, you can not play upon me.

SIGH NO MORE, LADIES SIGH NO MORE
MEN WERE DECEIVERS EVER.
ONE FOOT IN SEA AND ONE ON SHORE,
TO ONE THING CONSTANT, NEVER.
SIGH NOT SO, BUT LET THEM GO
AND BE YOU BLITHE AND BONNY,
CHANGING YOUR SOUNDS OF WOE TO HEY NONNY NONNY
SIGH NO MORE, LADIES SIGH NO MORE
MEN WERE DECEIVERS, EVER.
ONE FOOT IN SEA AND ONE ON SHORE
TO ONE THING CONSTANT, NEVER.

SING NO MORE DITTIES, SING NO MORE
OF DUMPS SO DULL AND HEAVY,
THE FRAUD OF MEN WAS SO SINCE SUMMER FIRST WAS
     LEAVY

SIGH NO MORE, LADIES SIGH NO MORE
MEN WERE DECEIVERS EVER.
ONE FOOT IN SEA AND ONE ON SHORE
TO ONE THING CONSTANT, NEVER.

SIGH NOT SO, BUT LET THEM GO
AND BE YOU BLITHE AND BONNY
CHANGING YOUR SOUNDS OF WOE TO HEY NONNY NONNY

SIGH NO MORE, LADIES SIGH NO MORE
MEN WERE DECEIVERS EVER.
ONE FOOT IN SEA AND ONE ON SHORE

TO ONE THING CONSTANT, NEVER.
TO ONE THING CONSTANT, NEVER.

We are wise girls to mock our lovers so. Where's my fool? Where's the knave?
PIANIST.   Where is that mongrel?

17

FOOL. *(Re-entering.)* I've been to the surgeon.

FEMALE SINGER. Come, a song ... and give it me in mine ear.

(Music #6: I Will Tarry)

FOOL.

> THAT SIR WHICH SERVES
> AND SEEKS FOR GAIN,
> AND FOLLOWS BUT FOR FORM,
> WILL PACK WHEN IT BEGINS TO RAIN
> AND LEAVE THEE IN THE STORM
> BUT I WILL TARRY
> THE FOOL WILL STAY
> AND LET THE WISE MAN FLY
> THE KNAVE TURNS FOOL
> THAT RUNS AWAY
> THE FOOL NO KNAVE

(Musical break.)

> BUT I WILL TARRY
> THE FOOL WILL STAY
> AND LET THE WISE MAN FLY
> THE KNAVE TURNS FOOL
> THAT RUNS AWAY
> THE FOOL NO KNAVE ...

I will tarry. The Fool will stay. *(Picks up Shakespeare puppet.)* Is thy name William? *(Puppet nods yes.)* Oh, tell me where is fancy bred, or in the heart, or in the head? It is engendered in the eyes.

PUPPET. A man may see how this world goes with no eyes.

FOOL. Look with thine ears. Lend me your ears. Bosom up my counsel, you'll find it wholesome. What is honor?

PUPPET. A word.

FOOL. What is that word, honor?

PUPPET. Air.

FOOL. Do you see how yon justice rails upon yon simple thief? *(Puppet nods.)* Hark in your ear.... Change places, and Handy Dandy. Which is the justice? Which is the thief?

PUPPET. The first thing we do let's kill all the lawyers.

18

FOOL.   Oh upright judge, oh learned judge. The quality of mercy is not strained. The rarer action is in virtue than in vengeance. Dost thou hear?

PUPPET.   Thy tale sir could cure deafness.

FOOL.   Thou hast seen a farmer's dog bark at a beggar ... and the creature run from the cur? *(Puppet nods.)* There thou mightst behold the great image of authority, a dog's obeyed in office. Robes and furred gown hide all. Through tattered clothes, small vices do appear. *(Puppet has exposed himself.)*

BAND MEMBER.   A bawd, a bawd...!

FOOL.   None does offend, none, I say none.

BAND MEMBER.   It offends me to the soul.

FOOL.   Take that of me my friend. *(Fool blows a "raspberry.")*

BAND MEMBER.   Thou darest wag thy tongue in noise so rude against me? I see your eyes are open, but their sense is shut.

FOOL.   Shall I get me glass eyes, and like a scurvy politician, seem to see the things he does not? I hold the world but as the world, a stage, where every man must play his part.

BAND MEMBER.   And yours a sad one ...

FOOL.   I, to the world am like a drop of water that, in the ocean, seeks another drop. I have of late, but wherefore I know not, lost all my mirth. Foregone all custom of exercise, and indeed, it goes so heavily ... *(Band Member crosses to clown and offers him a joint.)* What would you? What hempen homespun have we here? Weed ... wide enough to wrap a fairy in. Oh, wonderful, wonderful, and again most wonderful, and after that, out of all whooping. Oh, for a muse of fire. Give me some light, there. *(Audience member or Band Member lights a match.)* How far that little candle throws its beams. So shines a good deed in a naughty world. For this relief, much thanks. *(Lights the joint and takes a toke.)* Oh, true apothecary, thy drugs are quick! Oh, Jupiter, how merry are my spirits! *(To puppet.)* Do you see yonder cloud that's almost in shape like a camel? *(Puppet tokes and nods.)* Methinks tis like a weasel. *(Toke.)* Or like a whale. *(Both nod.)* What a piece of work is a man, man ... and admirable evasion of whoremaster man to lay his goatish disposition to the charge of a star. My father compounded with my mother under the dragon's tail, and my nativity was under Ursa Major, so that it follows, I am rough and lecherous.... Fut! Man delights not me, man. *(Puppet chuckles.)* No, nor woman, neither, though by your smiling you would seem to say so.

PUPPET.   There was no such stuff in my thoughts.

FOOL.   Why did you laugh, then when I said "man delights not me?"

PUPPET.   Because this weak and idle theme is no more yielding than a dream.

FOOL. I had a dream tonight.

PUPPET. And so did I.

FOOL. Well, what was yours?

PUPPET. That dreamers often lie!

FOOL. In bed asleep, where they do dream things true.

PUPPET. Oh, then I see Queen Mab hath been with you!

FOOL. Who?

PUPPET. Queen Mab!

FOOL. Who's she?

PUPPET. She's the fairies midwife, you fool ...

FOOL. Call you me fool? I do begin to perceive that I am made an ass.

PUPPET. Lord, what fools these mortals be!

FOOL. Lie thou there, thou block, thou stone, thou worse than senseless thing. *(Puts the puppet down.)* Thou art banished.

PUPPET. Banished?

FOOL. Thou wilt come no more.

PUPPET. Never?

FOOL. Never!

PUPPET. Never?

FOOL. Never!

PUPPET. Never?

FOOL. Never! The rest is silence. *(Beat.)* The time is out of joint. What country friend is this? For who would bear the whips and scorns of time?

(Music #7: Jazz)

Four-four time ... the oppressor's wrong, the proud man's contumely, the pangs of despised love ... love ... three-four time.... Oh, love, love, love.... Love is my sin — so are you to my thoughts as food to life. To life. To be or not to be ... to die.... Two-four time. Where the bee sucks there suck I.... Who would fardels bear?... What are fardels anyway?

MALE SINGER. A bundle, you fool.

FOOL. Well roared lion. To grunt and sweat under a weary life, but that the dread of something after death, the undiscovered country from whose bourne no traveller returns, puzzles the will, and makes us rather sit ... and let the sounds of music creep in our ears.

MALE SINGER. You speak all your part at once, man, cues and all. *(Fool picks up kazoo or other instrument.)* Note this before his note; there's not a note of his

20

worth the noting. *(Fool plays a solo.)*

FOOL.   Let me play the fool ... with mirth and laughter let old wrinkles come, and let my liver rather heat with wine than my heart cool with mortifying groans. *(Male Singer scats. Fool solos.)* Blow blow thou winter wind. Give us some music, good cousin sing. *(Male Singer scats. Fool solos.)* To each word a warbling note. I tell you what man, I love thee and it is my love that speaks. *(Male Singer scats. Sax and violin play.)* Blow winds and crack your cheeks, rage, blow and blows have answered blows. Speak frankly as the wind. Rage, Blow. *(Band plays.)* I'll tell thee more of this another time. *(Music ends. To the Puppet.)* Come, now, forget and forgive. We two will sing like birds in a cage.

HECKLER.   Nothing! Nothing!

FOOL.   What's this? What's this?

HECKLER.   Nothing, nothing, nothing!

FOOL.   Nothing will come of nothing, speak again?

HECKLER.   I marvel this audience takes delight in such a barren rascal.

FOOL.   Huh??

HECKLER.   Look you now.... Unless you laugh he is gagged.

FOOL.   Sir, why do you use me thus? I know you not.

HECKLER.   Fie, Fie. You counterfeit, you puppet you!

FOOL.   'Puppet?' Why, so — aye, that way goes the game! Now I perceive he hath made compare between our statures — He hath urged his height — What are you sir?

HECKLER.   Get you gone, you dwarf; You minimus, of hind'ring knotgrass made; You bead, you acorn!

FOOL.   'Little' again? Nothing but 'low' and 'little'!

PUPPET.   We are men, sir.

FOOL.   Speak for yourself.

HECKLER.   Be certain: nothing truer: 'tis no jest that I hate thee. You juggler. You canker blossom.

PUPPET.   I know you sir.

HECKLER.   What does thou know me for?

PUPPET.   A knave, a rascal, an eater of broken meats. A bull's pizzle!

FOOL.   A bull's pizzle?

PUPPET.   A bull's pizzle!

HECKLER.   Words, words, words..... Couple a word with a blow.

BAND MEMBER.   We'll have no brawling here!

FOOL.   I am no fighter sir. I am faint of heart that way, and he too.

HECKLER.   Thou woulds't quarrel with a man for having a hair more or a

21

hair less in his beard than thou hast. Thou woulds't quarrel with a man for cracking nuts, having no other reason but thou hast hazel eyes — Why appear you with this ridiculous boldness before my lady?

FEMALE SINGER.   When did I see thee so put down?

FOOL.   Never in your life I think.

HECKLER.   You're too old, sir, you're too old.

FOOL.   This same young sober blooded boy doth not love me nor a man cannot make him laugh.

HECKLER.   Are you a comedian?

FOOL.   I can say little more than I have studied, and that question's out of my part.

HECKLER.   You're a dry fool.

FOOL.   Give the dry fool drink, then is the fool not dry! *(Heckler produces a bottle of sack.)*

HECKLER.   Would you have a cup of sack, sir?

FOOL.   What, a rogue and peasant slave am I? Give be a *bottle* of sack. Why this is the best fooling when all is done. Let a cup of sack be my poison.

HECKLER.   *(Producing an egg.)* With egg, sir?

FOOL.   No, simple, of itself ... I'll put no pullet sperm in my brewage! *(Taking egg from the Heckler.)* What have we here? Sir Andrew Eggucheek ... *(Band boos.)* Young Fry of Treachery ... *(Band hisses.)* Omlette, Prince of Denmark ... *(Heckler produces a glass. Fool produces a much larger glass.)*

HECKLER.   I know thee by thy habits. Drunkenness is his best virtue. *(Fool pours and drinks a full glass.)*

FOOL.   A good sherry sack hath a two-fold operation in it. It ascends me to the brain and dries me there all the foolish, dull, and crudy vapors which environ it, makes it apprehensive, full of nimble, fiery, and delectable shapes, which given o'er to the voice, the tongue, which is the birth, becomes excellent wit. The second property of your excellent sherry *(He drinks a full glass.)* is the warming of the blood, which, before, cold and settled, left the liver white and pale, which is the badge of pusillanimity and cowardice ... but the sherry *(He drinks a full glass.)* warms it, and makes it course from the innards to the parts extreme. It illumineth the face, which, as a beacon, gives warning to the rest of this little kingdom, man, to arm. Then the petty inland spirits and vital commoners muster me all to their captain, the heart, who great and puffed up with this retinue, doth any deed of courage. And this valor comes of sherry ... *(He drinks a full glass.)* so that skill in the weapon is nothing without sack for that sets it a work ... and learning? A mere hoard of gold kept by a devil 'til sack commences it and puts it to act and use. If I had a thousand sons, the first humane principle I should teach them would be *(He produces a Diet Coke.)* to forswear thin potations, and to addict themselves to sack!

HECKLER.   Drink, sir, is the great provoker of three things.

FOOL.   What three things does drink especially provoke?

HECKLER.   Nose painting,

FOOL.   Hm, hm.

HECKLER.   Sleep,

FOOL.   Uh, huh.

HECKLER.   And urine.

FOOL.   Oooh ...

HECKLER.   Lechery, it provokes and unprovokes ...

FOOL.   How so?

HECKLER.   It provokes the desire, but takes away the performance.

FOOL.   I like thy wit well! This fellow is wise enough to play the fool. Come, come — A SONG! *(Music.)*

HECKLER.   My voice is ragged, I know I cannot please you.

FOOL.   I do not desire you to please me, I do desire you to sing.

HECKLER.   No, no, no.... This is a scurvy tune, to sing at a man's funeral.

FOOL.   Come, we'll do it together, like two old gypsies on a horse.

(Music #8: Let Her Go Hang)

THE HECKLER and THE FOOL.
>   THE MASTER, THE SWABBER, THE BOATSWAIN AND I
>   THE GUNNER AND HIS MATE
>   LOVED MALL, MEG, AND MARION
>   AND MARG'RY THE GREAT
>   BUT NONE OF US CARED FOR KATE.
>   FOR SHE HAD A TONGUE WITH A TANG,
>   SHE'D CRY TO A SAILOR "GO HANG"
>   SHE LOVED NOT THE SAVOR OF TAR
>   NOR OF PITCH;
>   YET A TAILOR MIGHT SCRATCH HER
>   WHERE'ER SHE DID ITCH.
>   THEN TO SEA, BOYS, AND LET HER GO HANG!

FOOL. The man that hath no music in himself, nor is not moved with concord of sweet sounds, is fit for treasons, stratagems, and spoils. The motions of his spirit are dull as night, and his affections dark ... let no such man be trusted ... mark the music!

(Music #9: Come Away Death)

MALE AND FEMALE SINGERS AND PIANIST.
> COME AWAY, COME AWAY DEATH
> AND IN SAD CYPRESS LET ME BE LAID
> FLY AWAY, FLY AWAY BREATH ...
> I AM SLAIN BY A FAIR CRUEL MAID.

PIANIST.
> MY SHROUD OF WHITE, STUCK ALL WITH YEW,

MALE AND FEMALE SINGERS AND PIANIST.
> OH PREPARE IT, OH PREPARE IT
> OH PREPARE IT, OH PREPARE IT
> OH PREPARE IT, OH PREPARE IT
> OH PREPARE IT, OH PREPARE IT

PIANIST.
> MY PART OF DEATH,
> NO ONE SO TRUE DID SHARE IT.

MALE AND FEMALE SINGERS AND PIANIST.
> NOT A FLOWER, NOT A FLOWER SWEET,
> ON MY BLACK COFFIN LET THERE BE STREWN.
> NOT A FRIEND, NOT A FRIEND GREET
> MY POOR CORPSE, WHERE MY BONES
> SHALL BE THROWN.

PIANIST.
> A THOUSAND, THOUSAND SIGHS TO SAVE.

MALE AND FEMALE SINGERS AND PIANIST.
>OH LAY ME, OH LAY ME
>OH LAY ME, OH LAY ME
>OH LAY ME, OH LAY ME
>OH LAY ME, OH LAY ME

PIANIST.
>SAD TRUE LOVE NEVER FIND MY GRAVE
>TO WEEP THERE.

MALE AND FEMALE SINGERS AND PIANIST.
>LA, LA LA LA LA
>LA, LA LA LA LA

FOOL. Thou see'st we are not all alone unhappy. This wide and universal theater presents more woeful pageants than the scene wherein we play.
MALE SINGER. All the world's a stage.
FOOL. And all the men and women merely players, and when we are born, we cry that we are come to this great stage of fools.
MALE SINGER. Is man no more than this?

(Music #10: When In Disgrace)

FOOL. This is the state of man.... Today he puts forth the tender leaves of hope, tomorrow blossoms, and bears his blushing honors thick upon him. The third day comes a frost, a killing frost, and when he thinks, good, easy man, full surely his greatness is a ripening, nips his root, and then he falls ... sans teeth, sans eyes, sans taste, sans everything ...

MALE SINGER.
>WHEN IN DISGRACE WITH FORTUNE AND MEN'S EYES
>I ALL ALONE BEWEEP MY OUTCAST STATE
>AND TROUBLE DEAF HEAVEN WITH MY BOOTLESS CRIES,
>AND LOOK UPON MYSELF, AND CURSE MY FATE,
>
>WISHING ME LIKE TO ONE MORE RICH IN HOPE,
>FEATURED LIKE HIM, LIKE HIM WITH FRIENDS POSSESSED,

DESIRING THIS MAN'S ART, AND THAT MAN'S SCOPE,
WITH WHAT I MOST ENJOY, CONTENTED LEAST,

YET, IN THESE THOUGHTS, MYSELF ALMOST DESPISING,
HAPLY I THINK ON THEE, AND THEN MY STATE,
LIKE TO THE LARK AT BREAK OF DAY ARISING
FROM SULLEN EARTH,
SINGS HYMNS AT HEAVEN'S GATE;

FOR THY SWEET LOVE REMEMB'RED SUCH WEALTH BRINGS
THAT THEN I SCORN TO CHANGE MY STATE WITH KINGS.
(Musical break.)
FOR THY SWEET LOVE REMEMB'RED SUCH WEALTH BRINGS
THAT THEN I SCORN TO CHANGE MY STATE WITH KINGS

FOOL.   This king has cured me!
FEMALE SINGER.   Not without cause!
MALE SINGER.   I was adored once, too ... *(Exits.)*
PIANIST.   Must I speak now? *(All nod.)* After a well graced actor leaves the stage, all eyes are idly bent on him who enters next.
FEMALE SINGER.   Thinking his prattle to be tedious?
PIANIST.   Tedious? Would you have a love song, or a song of good life?
FEMALE SINGER.   A love song, a love song! I care not for the good life.
FOOL.   Sing it! 'Tis no matter how it be in tune, so long it make noise enough.

(Music #11: I Know a Bank)

PIANIST.

I KNOW A BANK WHERE THE WILD THYME BLOW
WHERE OXSLIPS AND THE NODDING VIOLETS GROW
QUITE OVERCANOPIED WITH LUSCIOUS WOODBINE,
AND SWEET MUSKY ROSE ...
AND WITH EGLANTINE ...

THERE SLEEPS TITANIA SOMETIME OF THE NIGHT,
LULLED, IN THESE FLOWERS WITH DANCES AND DELIGHT
AND THERE THE SNAKE CASTS OFF HIS ENAMELLED SKIN,

WEEDS WIDE ENOUGH TO WRAP A FAIRY IN,
I KNOW A BANK WHERE THE WILD THYME BLOW
(Clarinet solo.)

THERE SLEEPS TITANIA SOMETIME OF THE NIGHT,
LULLED, IN THESE FLOWERS WITH DANCES AND DELIGHT
AND THERE THE SNAKE CASTS OFF HIS ENAMELLED SKIN
WEEDS WIDE ENOUGH TO WRAP A FAIRY IN,
WELL, I KNOW A BANK WHERE THE WILD THYME BLOW.
I KNOW A BANK WHERE THE WILD THYME BLOW.

MALE SINGER.   *(Re-entering.)* Very sweet and contagious! A mellifluous voice ...
PIANIST.   Nay, I can gleek upon occasion.
ALL.   Gleek!?
PIANIST.   Well, he gleeks with a better grace, but I do it more natural.
FOOL.   He hath songs for man or woman of all sizes ... like a barber's chair, that fits all buttocks ... the pin buttock, the quatch buttock, the brawn buttock, ... pastoral, comical ... tragical, historical, buttock, buttock, buttock, buttock.
FEMALE SINGER.   Peace, fool ... he has the prettiest love songs for maids.
PIANIST.   I was adored once, too. How dost thou like this tune?
FEMALE SINGER.   It gives a very echo to the seat where love is throned.
FOOL.   Seat? That's a bountiful answer.
FEMALE SINGER.   Nay, do not think I flatter ... I can call spirits from the vasty deep.

(Music #12: I Do Love Thee)

MALE SINGER.   And so can I!
FOOL.   But will they come when you do call for them? *(Exits.)*

FEMALE SINGER.

I AM A SPIRIT OF NO COMMON RATE,
THE SUMMER STILL DOTH TEND UPON MY STATE,
THEREFORE GO WITH ME ...
AND I DO LOVE THEE.

MALE AND FEMALE SINGERS:

    I WILL GIVE THEE FAIRIES TO ATTEND ON THEE,

    AND THEY WILL FETCH THEE JEWELS FROM THE DEEP,

    AND SING THEE ON TO BLESSED SLEEP,

    AND I DO LOVE THEE.

(Musical break.)

    I WILL PURGE THY MORTAL GROSSNESS SO

    THAT THOU'LT LIKE AN AIRY SPIRIT GO ...

    AND THOU SHALT STAY WITH ME,

    AND I DO LOVE THEE.

(Male Singer exits.)

(Music #13: How Should I Your True Love Know)

FEMALE SINGER.   What, I love? I was adored once too.

    HOW SHOULD I YOUR TRUE LOVE KNOW

        FROM ANOTHER ONE?

    BY HIS COCKLE HAT AND STAFF

        AND HIS SANDAL SHOON.

    WHITE HIS SHROUD AS THE MOUTAIN SNOW

    LARDED ALL WITH SWEET FLOWERS,

    WHICH BEWEPT TO THE GROUND DID NOT GO,

    WITH TRUE-LOVE SHOWERS.

(Music #14: Take O Take)

    TAKE O TAKE THOSE LIPS AWAY,

    THAT SO SWEETLY WERE FORSWORN;

    AND THOSE EYES THE BREAK OF DAY,

    LIGHTS THAT DO MISLEAD THE MORN:

    BUT MY KISSES BRING AGAIN, BRING AGAIN;

    SEALS OF LOVE, BUT SEALED IN VAIN

    SEALED IN VAIN.

(Violin solo.)

BUT MY KISSES BRING AGAIN, BRING AGAIN;
SEALS OF LOVE BUT SEALED IN VAIN,
SEALED IN VAIN.

Oh, My little body is aweary of this great world. *(Exits.)*
FOOL.   If music be the food of love, play on.

(Music #15: If Music Be the Food of Love Bit)

(Pianist plays refrain.) Give me excess of it, that, surfeiting, the appetite may sicken, and so die ... that strain again ... *(Pianist repeats phrase.)* It had a dying fall ... enough, no more. *(Music stops.)* 'Tis not so sweet now as it was before. Oh spirit of love, how quick and fresh art thou. I do much wonder that one man, seeing how much another man is a fool when he dedicates his behaviors to love will, after he hath laughed at such shallow follies in others, become the argument of his own scorn by falling in love. One woman is fair, yet I am well, another is wise, yet I am well, another is virtuous, yet I am well. But, 'til all graces be in one woman, one woman shall not come in my grace.... I will not love! If I do, hang me.... Oh, but her eye.... By this light, but for her eye, I would not love her ... yes, for her two eyes. Well, I do nothing in the world but lie, and lie in my throat ... I do love ... and it hath taught me to rhyme, and to be melancholy, and here *(Produces a letter.)* is part of my rhyme, and here ... *(Points to his heart.)* my melancholy. The lunatic, the lover, and the poet are of imagination all compact. One sees more devils than vast Hell can hold ... that is the lunatic. The lover, all as frantic, sees Helen's beauty in a brow of Egypt.... The poet's eye, in a fine frenzy rolling, doth glance from Heaven to Earth, from Earth to Heaven, and, as imagination bodies forth the forms of things unknown, the poet's pen turns them to shapes, and gives to airy nothing a local habitation and a name. Marry, I cannot find it in rhyme, I have tried. I can find out no rhyme for lady but baby *(Flute mock.)* an innocent rhyme ... for scorn, horn *(Sax mock.)* No, I was not born under a rhyming planet, nor I cannot woo in festival terms! What is this love? Is it a true thing? Love is merely a madness, and, I tell you, as well deserves a dark house and a whip as madmen do, and the reason why they are not so punished and cured is that the lunacy is so ordinary that the whippers are in love too ... and I, forsooth, in love! I, that have been love's whip, a very Beadle to an amorous sigh ... a nightwatch constable, a domineering pedant o'er the boy ... this wimpled, whin-

ing, purblind, wayward, boy, this senior, junior, giant, dwarf ... Dan Cupid....
And to love ... the worst of all ... a whitely wanton with a velvet brow, with two
pitch-balls stuck in her face for eyes ... and one that will do the "deed" though
argus were her guard.... And I to watch for her, to sigh for her, to pray for
her? It is a plague that Cupid will impose, for my neglect of his almighty, dread-
ful little might. Well ... I will write, sigh, pray, sue and groan. Some men must
love my lady, and some Joan.

(Music #16: Puck [Up and Down])

PIANIST.

    UP AND DOWN, UP AND DOWN,
    CUPID LEADS HIM UP AND DOWN;
    I AM FEAR'D IN FIELD AND TOWN;
    LOVE WILL LEAD HIM UP AND DOWN.
    HERE HE COMES.

FOOL. My mistress' eyes are nothing like the sun ... coral is far more red than
her lips are red. If snow be white, why then her breasts are dun: If hairs be
wires, black wires grow on her head. I have seen roses damask'd, red and white,
but no such roses see I in her cheeks, and in some perfumes is there more
delight than in the breath that from my mistress reeks. I love to hear her speak,
yet well I know that music hath a far more pleasing sound. I grant, I never saw
a Goddess go ... my mistress, when she walks, treads on the ground ... and yet,
by heaven, I think my love as rare as any she belied with false compare.

PIANIST.

    AND IN THE AIR, SLEEPING FAIR,
    I'LL APPLY TO YOUR EYE,
    GENTLE LOVER, REMEDY ...
    AND WHEN THOU WAK'ST,
    THOU TAK'ST,
    TRUE DELIGHT IN THE SIGHT
    OF THY FORMER LADY'S EYES ...

FOOL. But love ... first learned in a lady's eyes, lives not alone immured in
the brain, but with the motion of all elements, courses as swift as thought in

every power, and gives to every power a double power, above their functions and their offices. It adds a special seeing to the eye ... a lover's eye will gaze an eagle blind. A lover's ear will hear the lowest sound when the suspicious tread of theft is stopped. Love's feeling is more soft and sensitive than are the tender horns of cockled snails. Love's tongue proves dainty Bacchus gross in taste. For valor, is not love a Hercules, still climbing trees in the Hesperides? Subtle as Sphinx ... as sweet and musical as bright Apollo's lute, strung with his hair. Never durst poet touch a pen to write until his ink were tempered with love's sighs.... Oh, then his lines would ravish savage ears, and plant in tyrants mild humility. From women's eyes, this doctrine I derive ... they are the books, the arts, the academes that show, contain, and nourish all the world. And when Love speaks, the voice of all the Gods makes heaven drowsy with the harmony.

PIANIST.
> AND THE COUNTRY PROVERB KNOWN ...
> THAT EVERY MAN SHOULD TAKE HIS OWN ...
> IN YOUR WAKING SHALL BE SHOWN ...

FOOL.   Jack shall have Jill; naught shall go ill. The man shall have his mare again, and all shall be well. (*Exits.*)

(*Music #17:   O Mistress Mine*)

MALE SINGER.
> O MISTRESS MINE, WHERE ARE YOU ROAMING?
> O STAY AND HEAR, YOUR TRUE LOVE'S COMING
> THAT CAN SING BOTH HIGH AND LOW.
>
> TRIP NO FURTHER, PRETTY SWEETING,
> JOURNEY'S END IN LOVERS MEETING ...
> EVERY WISE MAN'S SON DOTH KNOW ...
>
> WHAT IS LOVE? 'TIS NOT HEREAFTER
> PRESENT MIRTH HATH PRESENT LAUGHTER ...
> WHAT'S TO COME IS STILL UNSURE ...
> WHAT'S TO COME IS STILL UNSURE ...

(*Musical break.*)

WHAT IS LOVE? 'TIS NOT HEREAFTER
PRESENT MIRTH HATH PRESENT LAUGHTER ...
WHAT'S TO COME IS STILL UNSURE ...
WHAT'S TO COME IS STILL UNSURE ...

IN DELAY THERE LIES NO PLENTY,
THEN COME KISS ME, SWEET AND TWENTY ...
YOUTH'S A STUFF WILL NOT ENDURE.
YOUTH'S A STUFF WILL NOT ENDURE.

(Music #18: Let Me Not)

FEMALE SINGER.
LET ME NOT TO THE MARRIAGE OF TRUE MINDS,
ADMIT IMPEDIMENTS.
LOVE IS NOT LOVE WHICH ALTERS
WHEN IT ALTERATION FINDS

OH, NO! IT IS AN EVER-FIXED MARK
THAT LOOKS ON TEMPESTS, NEVER SHAKEN,
IT IS THE STAR TO EVERY WANDERING BARK.

MALE SINGER.
LOVE'S NOT TIME'S FOOL, THOUGH ROSY LIPS AND CHEEKS
WITHIN HIS BENDING SICLE'S COMPASS COME.
LOVE ALTERS NOT WITH HIS BRIEF HOURS AND WEEKS,
BUT BEARS IT OUT EVEN TO THE EDGE OF DOOM.

FEMALE and MALE SINGERS.
OH, NO! IT IS AN EVER-FIXED MARK
THAT LOOKS ON TEMPESTS, NEVER SHAKEN,
IT IS THE STAR TO EVERY WANDERING BARK.
(Violin solo.)
IF THIS BE ERROR AND UPON ME PROVED,
I NEVER WRIT, NOR NO MAN EVER LOVED ...

OH, NO! IT IS AN EVER-FIXED MARK

THAT LOOKS ON TEMPESTS, NEVER SHAKEN,

IT IS THE STAR TO EVERY WANDERING BARK.

(Repeats.)

FOOL.   *(Entering.)* What a caterwauling do you keep here?

MALE SINGER.   All the better ... we shall be the more marketable!

FOOL.   Have you no respect of persons, place, nor time in you?

MALE SINGER.   We did keep time, sir, in our catches.... Sneck up! *(Exits.)*

ALL.   Sneck?

FEMALE SINGER.   You do look, my friend, in a moved sort, as if you were dismayed ... be cheerful, sir.

FOOL.   In sooth, I know not why I am so sad. It wearies me.

FEMALE SINGER.   They say you are a melancholy fellow.

FOOL.   It is so ... I do love it better than laughing ... I prithee, pretty youth, let me be better acquainted with thee, for though I look old, yet I am strong and lusty.

FEMALE SINGER.   Therefore your age is as a lusty winter ... frosty, but kindly?

FOOL.   I have neither the musician's melancholy, which is fantastical, nor the lady's, which is nice ... but it is a melancholy of mine own, compounded of many simples.

FEMALE SINGER.   I fear you have sold your own lands to see other men's.

FOOL.   True ...

(Music #19: That Time of Year)

and the sundry contemplation of my travels wraps me in a most humorous sadness ... but I will weary you no further with talking ...

THAT TIME OF YEAR THOU MAYST IN ME BEHOLD,

WHEN YELLOW LEAVES, OR NONE, OR FEW DO HANG

UPON THOSE BOUGHS WHICH SHAKE AGAINST THE COLD,

BARE RUINED CHOIRS, WHERE LATE THE SWEET BIRDS SANG.

IN ME THOU SEES'T THE TWILIGHT OF SUCH DAY,

AS AFTER SUNSET FADETH IN THE WEST,

WHICH BY AND BY BLACK NIGHT DOTH TAKE AWAY,
DEATH'S SECOND SELF, THAT SEALS UP ALL IN REST.

IN ME THOU SEES'T THE GLOWING OF SUCH FIRE,
THAT ON THE ASHES OF HIS YOUTH DOTH LIE,
AS THE DEATH-BED, WHEREON IT MUST EXPIRE,
CONSUMED WITH THAT WHICH IT WAS NOURISHED BY.
THIS THOU PERCEIVS'T, WHICH MAKES THY LOVE MORE
      STRONG,
TO LOVE THAT WELL, WHICH THOU MUST LEAVE ERE LONG.

FEMALE SINGER.   Age cannot wither you, nor custom stale your infinite variety.
FOOL.   You are full of pretty answers.

(Music #20: Shall I Compare Thee)

FEMALE SINGER.
      SHALL I COMPARE THEE TO A SUMMER'S DAY?
      THOU ART MORE LOVELY AND MORE TEMPERATE,
      ROUGH WINDS DO SHAKE THE DARLING BUDS OF MAY,
      AND SUMMER'S LEASE HATH ALL TOO SHORT A DATE.

      SOMETIME TOO HOT THE EYE OF HEAVEN SHINES,
      AND OFTEN IS HIS GOLD COMPLEXION DIMMED,
      AND EVERY FAIR FROM FAIR SOMETIME DECLINES,
      BY CHANCE, OR NATURE'S CHANGING COURSE UNTRIMMED;

      BUT THY ETERNAL SUMMER SHALL NOT FADE,
      NOR LOSE POSSESSION OF THAT FAIR THOU OW'ST,
      NOR SHALL DEATH BRAG THOU WAND'REST IN HIS SHADE,
      WHEN IN ETERNAL LINES TO TIME THOU GROW'ST.
(Violin solo.)
      SHALL I COMPARE THEE TO A SUMMER'S DAY?
      THOU ART MORE LOVELY AND MORE TEMPERATE.
      ROUGH WINDS DO SHAKE THE DARLING BUDS OF MAY.
      AND SUMMER'S LEASE HATH ALL TOO SHORT A DATE.

SO LONG AS MEN CAN BREATHE OR EYES CAN SEE,
SO LONG LIVES THIS, AND THIS GIVES LIFE TO THEE.

FOOL.   Madam, you have bereft me of all words ... only my blood speaks to you in my veins.
FEMALE SINGER.   ... and I, to the world, am like a drop of water ...
FOOL.   ... that in the ocean ...
FEMALE SINGER and FOOL.   ... seeks another drop.
MALE SINGER.   *(Re-entering.)* And yet, for aught I see, the course of true love never did run smooth ...

(Music #21: Love Is Perjured)

FEMALE SINGER.   But shall we make the welkin dance indeed?
FOOL.   Come on, let's have one more gaudy night!!!

MALE SINGER.
> LOVE IS PERJURED EVERYWHERE
> LOVE IS PERJURED EVERYWHERE
>
> OH, SERPENT HEART, WITH FLOWERING FACE,
> DID EVER DRAGON KEEP SO FAIR A CAVE?
> HONORABLE VILLAIN! DAMNED SAINT!
> LOVE IS PERJURED EVERYWHERE
> LOVE IS PERJURED EVERYWHERE

FEMALE SINGER.
> DOVE FEATHERED RAVEN, LAMB EATING WOLF,
> DIVINEST SUBSTANCE OF THE VILEST SHOW
> BEAUTIFUL TYRANT, FIEND ANGELICAL
> LOVE IS PERJURED EVERYWHERE
> LOVE IS PERJURED EVERYWHERE

FEMALE and MALE SINGERS.
> THERE IS NO TRUST, NO FAITH

FEMALE SINGER.
    NO HONESTY IN MEN.

FEMALE and MALE SINGERS.
    ALL FORSWORN, ALL HYPOCRITES,

MALE SINGER.
    BUT I'M A FOOL AGAIN

FEMALE and MALE SINGERS.
    LOVE IS PERJURED EVERYWHERE
    LOVE IS PERJURED EVERYWHERE
(Saxophone solo.)
    THERE IS NO TRUST, NO FAITH

FEMALE SINGER.
    NO HONESTY IN MEN.

FEMALE and MALE SINGERS.
    ALL FORSWORN, ALL HYPOCRITES,

MALE SINGER.
    AND I'M A FOOL AGAIN

FEMALE and MALE SINGERS.
    LOVE IS PERJURED EVERYWHERE
    LOVE IS PERJURED EVERYWHERE
    BEAUTIFUL TYRANT, FIEND ANGELICAL ...

    LOVE IS PERJURED EVERYWHERE
    LOVE IS PERJURED EVERYWHERE
(Repeats.)

FOOL.   The words of Mercury are harsh after the songs of Apollo. And now we few, we happy few, we band of brothers, for there is none of you so mean and base that hath not noble lustre in your eyes ... on mean bass ... *(Introduces the Bass Player.)* Another plucker of Cupid's bow strings ... here's his fiddlestick, here's that'll make you dance ... *(Introduces Violinist.)* Pray you, sir, are these wind instruments?

WOODWIND PLAYER.   Marry, they are, sir.

FOOL.   Well, blow 'til thou burst thy wind.

WOODWIND PLAYER.   I shall break my wind...!

FOOL.   Govern these ventages with your finger and thumb. Give it breath with your mouth and it will discourse most eloquent music. *(Introduces Woodwind Player.)* Who calls me villain? Plucks off my beard and blows it in my face? *(Introduces Heckler.)* O she doth teach the torches to burn bright. Why there's a wench. *(Introduces Female Singer.)* A great reckoning in a little room. The showing of a heavenly effect in an earthly actor. *(Introduces Male Singer.)* You "re" us, and "fa" us, you note us: and there is much music in this little organ ... *(Introduces Pianist.)*

PIANIST.   Brevity is the soul of wit. A very witty fool ... *(Introduces the Fool.)*

(Music #22:   Hey Ho Underscore)

FOOL.   The iron tongue of midnight hath tolled ... *(Looks at his watch, says whatever time it is.)* Lovers, ... to bed ... 'tis almost fairy time ... and these our actors, as I foretold you, were all spirits and are melted into air, into thin air ... we are such stuff as dreams are made on ... and I have had a most rare vision ... I have had a dream past the wit of man to say what dream it was ... methought I had ... methought I was ... but man is a patched fool if he will offer to say what methought I had ... I will get Ray Leslee to write a ballad of this dream ... and so we'll live, and sing, and pray, and laugh at gilded butterflies, and hear poor rogues talk of court news, and we'll talk with them, too. Who's in, who's out, who loses and who wins ... and we'll speak what we feel, not what we ought to say.... And take upon us the mystery of things, as if we were God's spies.

(Music #23:   Hey Ho)

> WHEN THAT I WAS AND A LITTLE TINY BOY
> WITH HEY HO, THE WIND AND THE RAIN,
> A FOOLISH THING WAS BUT A TOY,
> FOR THE RAIN IT RAINETH EVER DAY.

PIANIST.

    BUT WHEN I CAME TO MAN'S ESTATE

    WITH HEY HO, THE WIND AND THE RAIN,

    'GAINST KNAVES AND THIEVES MEN SHUT THEIR GATE,

    FOR THE RAIN IT RAINETH EVERY DAY.

(Musical break.)

MALE SINGER.

    BUT WHEN I CAME ALAS TO WIVE

    WITH HEY HO, THE WIND AND THE RAIN,

    BY SWAGGERING COULD I NEVER THRIVE,

    FOR THE RAIN IT RAINETH EVERY DAY.

FEMALE SINGER.

    BUT WHEN I CAME UNTO MY BEDS,

    WITH HEY HO, THE WIND AND THE RAIN,

    WITH TOSSPOTS STILL HAD DRUNKEN HEADS,

    FOR THE RAIN IT RAINETH EVERY DAY.

(Musical break.)

FOOL.

    A GREAT WHILE AGO, THE WORLD BEGUN,

ALL.

    WITH HEY HO, THE WIND AND THE RAIN,

FOOL.

    BUT THAT'S ALL ONE, OUR PLAY IS DONE,

ALL.

    AND WE'LL STRIVE TO PLEASE YOU EVERY DAY.

FOOL.   Our revels now are ended. Thanks to you all and leave us.... You that way, ... we this way.

CURTAIN

PROPERTY LIST

Shakespeare puppet (FOOL)
Joint (BAND MEMBER)
Matches
Bottle of sack (HECKLER)
Drinking glass (HECKLER)
Larger drinking glass (FOOL)
Diet Coke (FOOL)
Letter (FOOL)
Wristwatch (FOOL)